Being Still

A Journal of Reflection and Renewal

Kayla L. Westra

Dedication: This book is dedicated to my family, all of whom show me the goodness of God's love every day. Also, to my friends who struggle, worship, and praise with me; your faith and understanding are invaluable. Thank you all for walking with me on this journey.

Bible Verses: I used singular verses as a focus for these devotionals. Single verses are powerful and easier to remember. Focusing on single verses does have a drawback, and that is you will not get the complete context of the verse within its book and chapter. I encourage you to read the verses surrounding the ones I've focused on for more depth of understanding.

Photographs: All photographs in this book are the property of the author. Many of these were taken in Ireland and Scotland, and some were taken within my yard. God's beauty abounds!

Translations: I used multiple translations to create this journal. You'll find most often the *Good News Bible*, *The Message*, and *New International Version*.

Thank you!

Thank you for supporting an independent author. If you enjoyed this devotional, **please leave a review** on your favorite site (Amazon, Goodreads, Bookbub, etc.).

Kayla L Westra

AUTHOR

Table of Contents

Introduction: Reflection and Renewal Through Being Still

Be still? Be STILL? As a young person, the idea of being still didn't appeal to me. If I was going to make my way in the world, I needed to do something. Anything. Keep moving forward, keep climbing, keep learning, keep going. Don't ever stop. I wasn't content to just be still. God helps those who help themselves, right? He'll do His part if I do mine? There may be some truth in both of those maxims. But now that I'm older, and hopefully, a bit wiser, I feel for that young woman.

Before the turn of the millennia in 2000, the "you can be whatever you want to be" mantra was in full force. But the reality then, and even now, is that isn't true. For those who are privileged, this mantra is much more likely to be true. Hard work and perseverance can change one's situation in many cases. I may have taken that idea to the extreme, as did my husband. We worked hard, saved, planned, and drove ourselves to achieve. Now, at a time in our careers when we no longer need to push and drive and achieve…I wonder why it was so hard to reset my thought processes and refocus on joy, thankfulness, and life. Not that I haven't always been thankful - I am blessed beyond measure. However, I had (have?) a hard time finding joy. Work became too much of my life, and though I knew better, it still happened, and not to positive results. How do you extricate your identity from what you do? How do you really live?

I wrote this renewal journal during my process of renewal, and then revised to make it more applicable for those who might want to undertake a similar journey. There's no right or wrong way to complete this devotional, but I recommend thinking through how you will complete this to get the most out of the materials for your growth. We've all bought journals and not completed them; the ones that were truly helpful, I read and wrote through the last page. As an English teacher, I always told my students to learn to write, because some day, there'd be something they would want to say. I hope I have accomplished that here. There's also no singularly focused audience in mind for this journal; this devotional likely has appeal to all ages, all career stages, and all genders.

I'm hopeful you will find this material to be helpful for you, wherever you are in your journey. Figure out your own plan, whether it is to complete this in a week, a month, six months, or whatever timeframe you determine best for you to work through these writings. Maybe you'd like to encourage your Bible study group to add this journal to their study or complete this with trusted friends. Maybe you prefer working through this on your own. Whatever you decide, I'll challenge you to complete this journal. You may find that some of the writing prompts are difficult; if you need to come back to them, do that, but don't stop moving forward. I know, I know. This book is about being still, right? My advice is don't be still too long, and never in your relationship with God. When we understand ourselves, we understand more about our purpose, our passion, and our belonging. We are better equipped to focus on what He wants us to do, and not so much on the daily noise each of us encounters.

Belonging is a key tenet to my faith. I am a child of God, a daughter of the King. You are a child of God as well, and you belong in His family. You are worthy of peace, of love, of stillness, and of joy. I am so very grateful that God does not keep track of our mistakes, nor does He measure us by our failings. Enjoy this reflection and renewal, and I am praying that you'll find your joy through the process. Focus on becoming the best version of you, God's version of you, as you head down this path.

Kayla L. Westra

1 Be still and know that I am God (Psalm 46:10)

Being still has always been tough for me. From a very young age, I was a rocker. Maybe you were too or you knew someone who was. Oh, and I should probably be clear about this; I was not the cool kind of rocker. I didn't play in a band. No, I rocked myself to sleep at night. I rocked in the car when we traveled. I don't remember when I first realized that I was rocking myself to sleep, but I can remember shifting in my small bed, soothing myself to sleep. Growing up on a small farm where there was limited TV programming inside and animals outside, you can guess, I was outside and in motion all day long, and it seemed that I couldn't stop being in motion when it was time for bed. During the day, I was busy. Finding kittens in the hay mow. Brushing my pony. Trekking through the grove with my trusty farm dog, Gomer. I was on the go, even in the harsh Minnesota winters. Bread bags over my feet to keep the snow and damp out of my leaky boots, I was outside until my hands and feet hurt, until my lips were dry and my cheeks red. It was no surprise, then, that at night, I had a hard time being still and resting.

I rocked in the car, too. I'd sit in the middle of the sedan, feet on the "hump," in between my two brothers, and I'd rock. Didn't matter if we were going two miles or two hundred miles, I was in motion while the car was in motion. Dad joked that we went two miles forward, one mile back. I don't remember my parents telling me to sit still. They probably did, but I don't recall being scolded. In school, I was wiggly. I could sit still; I just preferred not to (Bartleby, anyone?). Best time of the school day? Moving from our classroom to the library, or to lunch, or best yet, recess, where I could be in motion.

No surprise, then, that I was an athlete and rode horses. More motion. More getting from here to there. If we were visiting family, I had to come inside and eat, then visit for a half hour. After making an appearance, I was allowed to change clothes and go outside. That did frustrate my mom, I can remember that. Why couldn't I stay in and play with dolls or a tea set? Even my one sedentary hobby caused friction. I read voraciously, everything I could get from the school library. I may have been seated and reading, but my mind was in motion, exploring through the words on the page. Summers were tough - no books - but then I had the outdoors.

While it wasn't my first job, it was early in my career, and my mentor (and friend, 30+ years later), coached me on how to be a better writer and editor. Her skill in that regard was legendary. But it was another piece of wisdom that she imparted that had more impact. "Be still," she'd say. "Sometimes no action is a response." But, but, but…. I was used to being in motion, to making things happen, to shaping my life in the ways that I wanted it to go. I knew the rest of that verse, too, but I liked to ignore it, if I am being honest with myself. "Be still and know that I am God." She wasn't just telling me to slow down, to consider things more fully before acting. The guidance was bigger than that; she wanted me to be still and let Him handle things. It took me years to get to that lesson, and sometimes, even now, I need to remind myself that I don't always have to be in motion or solve every problem. It is absolutely okay to be still and let God be God.

Prayer: Lord, help us to be aware of our need to be in motion, and when we should instead be still and wait on You. Keep our eyes on You so that we keep our priorities straight. In our stillness, may we listen for Your voice. Help us to know that You are God, and we don't need to be in control, that You want to bless us and keep us safe. Amen.

 **Writing** Is it hard for you to be still? Why do you think that is? What do you want to do differently moving forward? If you do not have an issue with being still, what have you learned in the stillness? How has this ability to be still served you well?

Be still, and know that I am God. Psalm 46:10

_____

_____

_____

_____

_____

_____

_____

_____

_____

_____

_____

_____

_____

_____

_____

2 Why so downcast? (Psalm 42:11)

It is no surprise to anyone reading this devotional that life is sometimes really hard. Messy. Unpredictable. And the worst - unfair. Accidents happen, diagnosis are made, or a life is cut short or irrevocably changed. It can be difficult to be joyful, grateful, and praising in the midst of life's storms and trials.

The summer before sixth grade, our family went on a vacation. We often camped or visited relatives - nothing too extravagant. Sometimes our extended family went with us. For farm families, there are small windows of time where a grain farmer can step out and take a rest before harvest begins, and I imagine that's why we took a trip that August. We returned home on a Sunday, and Monday, my father went in to help move grain at the local elevator. My dad was a hard worker; if there was work available off the farm to supplement the income, he took those jobs.

That Monday changed our lives. Dad went in to work, and he had just dumped a load of grain and was walking out the big elevator doors when one of the workers flipped the switch so the corn would be processed. The resulting explosion threw Dad 100 feet into the street. The heat from the blast melted his mostly polyester shirt into his skin, and he was badly burned. I remember the neighbors coming to tell Mom what had happened. I sat at the

11

top of the steep staircase in the old farmhouse and listened. "Gordon was burned - they are taking him by ambulance to the burn unit in the Twin Cities." I'd find out later that Dad didn't think he was injured badly enough to go in the ambulance; he was more worried about the two men who were inside the elevator. Four months in a burn unit, with second and third degree burns over 60 percent of his body, and Dad finally came home at Thanksgiving. I'd only seen him once in those 16 weeks; my mom didn't come home during that time, that I recall. I stayed with an aunt and uncle; neighbors took care of the harvest that year.

And my dad was able to come home. My classmate's dad did not. The explosion forever changed many families in the area. Dad's prognosis, I'd find out later, wasn't very good. He had been given a 10 percent chance of recovery. His burns had healed, mostly, but the damage to his lungs was an unknown. He lived 37 years after that, far exceeding the doctor's expectations. And Dad's faith was stalwart through this trial. I know there were bad days, even after he came home. Healing skin itches terribly and wearing the Jobst suit was not comfortable. Dad couldn't work, but he could laugh, he could sing, he could praise, and he could help others. Watching those lessons during my formative years made an impact on me as an adult. If Dad could keep his sense of humor after what he'd gone through, if he could keep his faith and even strengthen his faith after that life-changing event, so could I. We all

12

have stories, things that shaped us, things that changed us. It is not difficult to get an invitation to a pity party; the hard part is knowing when to leave. Larnelle Harris talks about choosing joy in one of his songs; it is definitely a choice!

Psalm 42:11 reminds us that we can put our hope in God; He won't let us down, regardless of what happens to us. Our souls know that He is with us, that He has a plan, and that we do not need to be downcast, sad, defeated, or distraught. We can put our trust in Him for a brighter tomorrow.

Prayer: Heavenly Father, help us to recognize our joys and our sorrows, and to put our faith and trust in You. We will be downcast during our lives, Lord, but we know that if we shift the focus from ourselves to You, that if we share our burdens with You, our burden will be lighter. Help us to think about our joys and to count our blessings daily. Amen.

Writing: What brings me joy? This was a difficult question for me at my lowest. What DID bring me joy? My family - always. That never waned. But work? Friends? Simple things? What brings you joy? What used to bring you joy that you miss? How can you put your hope in God so that you can find your joy?

Why, my soul, are you downcast? Why so disturbed within me? Put your hope in God, for I will yet praise Him, my Savior and my God.

Psalm 42:11

_____

_____

_____

_____

_____

_____

_____

_____

_____

_____

_____

_____

_____

_____

3 Where does my help come from? (Psalm 121:1)

Servant leaders are those who are focused on helping others, regardless of title or position. These are the helpers; the people who look for ways to provide what is needed, often before someone can ask for help. True servant leaders often struggle with accepting help from others, even from God. I struggle with asking for help, even from my family. I really struggle asking for help from friends. And to be honest, I don't like asking God for help, either. For me, it is about being a burden to anyone else. Does this sound familiar?

Think about your circles - who is closest to you and who you turn to for help. These circles are rings about your person, with the closest ring including people who are closest to you. That first ring is often quite small. Maybe your parents are in that first ring. Or a spouse. A sibling. Your children. Maybe your best friend. Move out to the next circle. Who is in that ring? People you work with? Acquaintances? Cousins? Brene Brown talks about these concentric rings in her book, *Dare to Lead*. There are the people who are very close to you, and these are often those who you turn to for advice and help.

The first time I did this exercise when learning about Brene Brown's work, I made a huge omission in my first ring. I'd left out

God. Seriously. How could that even be? But like me, some of you may tend to compartmentalize work. We keep our faith life and our work life separate. Sometimes because it is an expectation. But sometimes, maybe, it is because we think we can control our work environment, or our families, or our home life, and that we really don't need to put God in those circles, because He's there anyway, right? Anyone? Following my logic? No?

Well, I hope your brain stopped here, and thought, what is she talking about? There was no logic in my separating God from my work life, but I had managed to leave God out of a major part of my day. I have a distinct memory of wearing a cross pendant to work one day, and a colleague made a disparaging remark about my necklace. I should have held true to my beliefs and my faith, but I was knocked off my pins, to use an old expression. Blindsided by the criticism. And so I didn't wear that necklace again, and I didn't outwardly bring my faith to work with me. That is hard to admit, but it's honest. This episode happened before the *Dare to Lead* work, and now, I know better than to take criticism from someone who is not in those circles mentioned above. I know better than to allow someone I would not go to for advice influence my behaviors.

That was then. Now, I know that my help is in the Lord, and I look to the hills, knowing where my help comes from. I live on the prairie, so the actual hills are not terribly pronounced. But He is there in the sunrises and sunsets, which are spectacular. He's there in the wild roses that grow in the ditch in summer. He's there in the wind that some days feels relentless. He's there as the farmland comes to life.

While it may be true that He is always there, and He knows what is in our hearts before we ask, my awareness of my lapse was a wake-up call. Was I taking for granted that God would be there? Was I praising Him in ways that honored Him, by acknowledging the things that He is capable of doing? Was I putting too much emphasis on my work? (The answer to that was yes, in case you were wondering.) We are enamored of the American Dream, that you can do anything, if you want it enough and work hard enough to achieve it. But is that mantra really honoring God? If we are believers, we know that He has promised us blessings upon blessings. So why do we fall for the lie that we can, on our own, achieve dreams that may or may not be God-given dreams? I know where my help comes from; I can trust Him to lead my life and to fulfill the plan that He has for me.

Prayer: Lord, help me to lean not on my power and my thoughts. Help me to focus on Your goodness and ask You for the help I need. May I keep Your praises at the forefront knowing that You have a good and Godly plan for my life. When I need help, Lord, I will run to You first. I will gladly lean on Your strength and love. Amen.

Writing: Who is in your first circle? How about your next ring? Do you take things to God? Right away? Or after you've told everyone in your circle, vented to your spouse, and complained to your sibling? Where does the Bible say our help comes from? Why are we so resistant to going to God to be lifted up? How can you approach this differently in the future?

I lift up my eyes to the mountains; where does my help come from?
Psalm 121:1

_____

_____

_____

_____

_____

_____

_____

_____

_____

_____

_____

_____

_____

4 I will be content in all circumstances (Philippians 4:11)

Oh, this is a tough one for me. You too? I am so blessed and so grateful; I have a wonderful family, wonderful friends, and a wonderful life. And I also can complain with the best of them over the one thing that is stealing my joy. And when that thing is gone, I'm likely to pick up something else that is a struggle. I know I do it, and I know I don't want to repeat this behavior, but it is a struggle. As an example, I struggled when my daughters were playing high school sports. I'd been an athlete, and though we never had a winning team at my tiny high school, playing sports and being involved with the others on my team are some of the best memories of that experience. It wasn't about winning. It really wasn't even about being the best on the team, or scoring the most points, or having the best stat line. It was about having something to do, hanging out with friends, learning skills, and playing. Literally, playing. Some of my best memories were playing sports.

When my daughters started in sports, my viewpoint was skewed. I had coached when I taught junior high and high school. We'd worked hard, but we focused on having fun, being good teammates, and enjoying the games. Something had changed in that window between when I'd played and coached. And it seemed to be pervasive to the region. Winning was everything. I watched

23

year after year as kids were quitting after ninth or tenth grade, after being told by their coach that they weren't good enough to play for the team any longer. Really? Not good enough for small town teams, where every five years, one of the players might go play at the next level? This mentality drove me a bit crazy, and I was not my best self. I will admit, at games, I sometimes lost my cool. I was glad to see my girls either decide to move on to other pursuits or accept that this was how it was going to be.

Near the end of the season one year, I rode to an out-of-town game with a friend. On the way home, I apologized to her for my attitude. She was surprised; she hadn't noticed at all. "Well," I said, "at least all of that raging was going on in my mind and not coming out of my mouth." We laughed, but it was a defining moment for me. What if I had said all of what I had been thinking? How would that have helped the situation? And more importantly, how would that have shown who I am? How would my discontent and anger spill over into other areas of my life?

I'm reminded that when Paul wrote his letter to the Philippians, he was in prison. He wasn't traveling the world, staying in posh hotels and seeing the sights. He was being hounded for his faith and literally thrown in prison for it. The apostle Paul reminds us that regardless of our circumstances, regardless of how we feel at the moment, we should learn to be content. I'll keep working on that; and I hope you will join me!

Prayer: Lord, help me to focus on Your goodness and mercy, and not on the trivial things that steal my joy. Remind me to focus on grace, for myself and for others. Help me to praise more than I grumble. I can, Lord, be content, in all circumstances, with Your help. Amen.

Writing: What makes you discontented? Have you taken time to think about those things? Write them down? Do so now. Write down all the things that steal your joy, make you grumpy, or even make you angry. What patterns do you see? What things are true issues and need to be handled? What things are trivial and unimportant? And which of these items are just figments of your imagination and not real at all, once you take time to think about them? How will your reaction to these things change moving forward? What can you give to God?

I am not saying this because I am in need, for I have learned to be content whatever the circumstances.
Philippians 4:11

5 He uses all things for good (Romans 8:28)

Here's an uncomfortable truth; sometimes this verse annoys me. How can some of the awful, life-changing, life-ending things that happen be used for God's good? Wouldn't a compassionate God show compassion for everyone? Then why do people get cancer and die? Why are there accidents? Why are people victims of crimes? Why, as the song suggests, do only the good die young?

My husband has owned and operated a small-town restaurant for over 20 years. In addition to the long-term, full-time staff, every year, he hires 15-20 high school age employees. Many of these people have become family. Not like family. *Family*. They are great, not because they are or were awesome employees (many have been), but because they were good humans. We've gone to countless graduations, weddings, and unfortunately, some funerals.

And for one of these young people who has been family, she lost her life to cancer at age 35. Her first bout with cancer happened when she was in college. She fought that battle and won. Heather lost her mom soon after her remission. As a mother, it was hard for me to watch her grieve for her mom. Heather was blessed in meeting the love of her life and having two children. And then the cancer came back, with a vengeance. Those last months were tough, on her, on her husband, and certainly on her young children. And now she's gone. How can that possibly be for God's good? Heather had a strong faith, and she knew she was going to her eternal home. But for those of us who are left here on Earth, we are left wondering what could God's purpose be? Some will say that God called her home because he needed her in heaven. I can't speak for God, so I can't and won't speculate on His plan. But some of us are angry. We may not say it to others, but I've said it, and directly to God. Why Heather? She'd had so much to deal with in her young life, and now her husband and children, her dad, were left behind. How could her loss be for God's good? How do her family, her friends, reconcile her loss?

I know there are some who think we shouldn't question God. But I think He can take it. He can take our questions, our anger, and our hurt. He can take our rage at injustices, at the unfairness of life in an imperfect world, at the confusion we feel when a loved one's life is cut short. God is a big God. He isn't going to get mad at us when we tell Him how we feel. He wants to help us with our burdens; he wants to carry our hurts, our anger, our shame.

Christians know (or should know) that we will have trials throughout our lives. The apostle Paul reminds us of this, many times. Life isn't going to be easy. We are going to face hardships, difficult times, and grief. Paul reminds us to be content where we are, in all circumstances. Know that God uses all things for good. Know that we can't begin to know His purpose and His plan for our lives. We want to think that we are the masters of our destiny. But we aren't, regardless of how much we think we are in control. I will never know God's plan, or why he chose to take Heather home when he did. But I am coming to terms with the idea that His plan is outside of my ability to understand, and I can honor her memory by telling her story and remembering her smile.

Leadership experts talk about flipping the script, and rather than thinking about why something bad has happened to us, to think about what we can learn from the experience. This idea can help us to focus on the growth and the learning, and to think about ways that God may be using what is happening to us, right now, as part of His larger plan. Heather was a fighter. She loved her family and friends dearly. She was a living example of God's love. We can all hope to be remembered in a similar way. We can honor her memory in many ways.

Prayer: God, comfort us when we lose loved ones and help us to remember that our life here on Earth is temporary. We will face trials. We will have hard times. But that doesn't mean we have to be discontent. The apostle Paul reminds us that You are working for our good, and that we can remain steadfast in the knowledge that You have a perfect plan. Amen.

Writing: How do you turn to God when hard things shake your foundation? What is a circumstance that you can think of and how did you handle it? In the future, how might you turn to God in a different way? How might you help others who are going through a difficult time? Finding the right words can be hard, especially when someone is hurting. What are some ways that you can be empathetic and show compassion to people?

And we know that in all things God works for the good of those who love him, who have been called according to his purpose.
Romans 8:28

6 My burden is light (Matthew 11:30)

I loved growing up on a farm and being from a small town. I didn't know anything different, but I loved being a farm kid. I was outside as much as I could be. And on a farm, there is always work to be done. A working farm may or may not be diversified in today's era. But farms in my childhood were nearly all diversified, meaning you had more than one revenue stream. In farming, that means crops and animals. For our family, that meant extended family (aunts, uncles, cousins) were involved in the operation, and we had beef cattle, dairy cattle, and horses, in addition to crops and an outside business.

When it was time to plant in the spring, everyone helped. You helped with tasks according to your age, and while the driving age in Minnesota was 15 for a farm permit, most of us were driving much earlier than that. Sometimes your job was as simple as picking up seed sacks and taking care of the trash; other times you might be helping take lunch out to the field or drive into town for parts. All chipped in in their own way.

If you had animals, as we did, there were chores. Morning and night. Automatic feeding systems weren't available yet, or maybe they were, and we just couldn't afford them. Cows and horses like to eat. On time. Every meal. You may not know this, but if you don't feed dairy cows what they need, when they need it, you negatively impact the milk production, which then impacts your profits. Dairy cows aren't very fond of strangers around the barn, either, which meant you didn't have random people feeding them. We also had 50 head of Arabian horses, and the minute the back door of the house opened, it was a symphony of whinnies and moos, everyone asking for their breakfast. If the dog was in the barn and not waiting on the back step, he'd be barking his greeting as well as he ran across the yard. The barn cats were camped on the back step; they knew their morning food came from the person coming out of the house. This animal four-part chorus repeated itself around five in the afternoon.

The cows were fairly easy to feed. Throw the food in the bunkers, be sure the hay was accessible and water tanks were full, and you could call it good. But with that many horses, that was a lot of feed to carry. Horses aren't self-feeders; we had to pay more attention to who got what rations. Three hundred sixty-five days of the year, this work goes on, and in all sorts of weather. Did I mention I grew up in Minnesota on the prairie? I schlepped a lot of miles carrying two five-gallon pails full of grain, pulled from the bin in the middle of the yard, and going to the various barns and pastures, often in less-than-ideal weather. Those pails were heavy. The hay bales we carried were 50-75 pounds, depending on the density and type of hay. At least the hay was stored in each barn. I didn't need to lift weights in those days. I was always glad when my best friend was around and could help fetch and carry. Feeding time was more fun when we were together, and we could get twice as much done with two pairs of hands. We shared the yoke of chores, and the burden was lighter. On summer nights, we sometimes goofed around, rode untrained pasture horses without even a halter, and enjoyed the long Minnesota days. But when it was below zero and the winter winds were howling, you appreciated not spending as much time outside. Having someone to help carry the load was pretty important.

Things are lighter when we help each other carry them. We know this intuitively. We can't lift a couch on our own or move other heavy furniture or appliances by ourselves. We count on our friends, our family, or hired help to help us carry things we can't carry by ourselves. This is true in our spiritual lives as well. Having a trusted friend (or five) you can turn to when your life is heavy is a blessing. Being that friend for another person is also a blessing. Knowing that God is there for us, every day, to listen to our concerns, our fears, our worries, is a central tenet of believers.

Prayer: Lord, thank You for always being there to listen to us. When we don't have the words, You hear what is in our hearts. Help us to turn to You first. Help us to be a blessing to others who are in need. Help us to share our burdens with others, and to listen to those who need compassion. Amen.

Writing: God tells us to give him our burdens. In fact, He says to give over the burdens and to let Him carry them. He doesn't say to hand them over and keep hanging on to them. How well do you follow these instructions? Describe your process of giving things to God. Do you pray about it? Do you physically write things down and put them in a prayer jar? What could you do better in this area? What has helped you the most in giving things to God?

For my yoke is easy, and my burden is light. Matthew 11:30

_____

_____

_____

_____

_____

_____

_____

_____

_____

_____

_____

_____

7 What do I want? (Psalm 27:4)

I think it is safe to say we all have bumps in our careers. Sometimes those bumps are black holes, and we are lucky to move through those trials with all our faith and confidence intact. I'd been working with a professional coach for a while when he hit me with that question at a particularly difficult time in my career. I was burned out. And he's asking me, what did I want. I knew what I didn't want. But what did I want? And why was that question so hard to answer? This Psalm makes all that wanting and worrying seem for naught: "I have asked the Lord for one thing; one thing only do I want: to live in the Lord's house all my life, to marvel there at his goodness and to ask his guidance." Getting back to this idea helped me recenter.

We live in a materialistic society. This is not news to most Americans, though even those who know seem to buy in to the culture, literally. Buy, buy, buy. Get that latest phone. How about the cool car? Vacation? Yes, please. And be sure to buy in bulk. March 2020 aside, you never know when you are going to need cases of toilet paper on hand. More is better. Even more is even more better. And yes, I know that last sentence isn't grammatically correct. The concept is what matters here. Bigger, better, costlier, more, more, more.

Being aware of this ideal is pretty important. We are buying into a philosophy that will never make us happy. Buying more, having more, doesn't bring peace. The simplicity of Psalm 27, verse 4, is its strength. If we focus on God's word and our place in His house, what more could we want? We can go to Him for counsel. We can ask for wisdom and advice. He has promised to take care of our needs. If we are living with Christ, what more could we want?

As a farm kid from a very small town, with a dad who'd been injured and no longer able to work, you can guess that we didn't have a lot of money. I recognize scarcity mentality when I see it because I've lived it. I didn't want for anything; I was loved, I was able to show horses (which I also loved), and I was blessed in countless ways. As I moved away as an adult, and money was scarce for us as a young, newly married couple, I recognized the scarcity mentality in myself. Even now, more than 35 years later, I have to use my rationale brain to overcome those feelings. I have been blessed beyond measure. But it's important to remember; money is just money. It isn't happiness. It never will be. Again, that's a privileged viewpoint, and I recognize that.

My dad was one of the most generous people I've ever met, and I'm so thankful for his lessons in that regard. He would joke about there not being pockets in coffins, referencing that you can't take your money and possessions with you. And we had a good laugh at a hard time when we were choosing my mom's coffin; Dad's surprise that there were in fact pockets in coffins made us both laugh. He was still generous and loved to give, much more than he liked to receive.

Refocusing our wants and viewing our lives through God's lens can help us see our excesses, our reliance on things, and help us to modify, if we want, how we approach life. The question, perhaps, is do we want to go against the norms of American culture? I have a thing for books. I'm going to keep buying books. But I'm changing some of the other things I buy, either cutting them out completely or buying less. I just don't need things anymore. And I know that that is a very privileged viewpoint. I am blessed and I have plenty. I have more than plenty. I can do without. The key is, where I can help others, I'm stepping out to do that. I often think, how can I honor my dad's generosity by being generous to others?

Prayer: Heavenly Father, we ask You for wisdom and guidance when it comes to things and possessions. Help us to focus not on excess but on others, sharing Your love and giving our time, talents, and resources to make a difference in their lives. Regardless of my circumstances, Lord, help me to see where I can be generous, with my money, my time, and my abilities. Push me, Lord, to be a beacon of light. Amen.

Writing: If you take a look at your habits, where do you have excess? Why do you think that is? If you were to get rid of that excess, what would happen? How can you lean into God's security and His wisdom when it comes to materialism? How can you help others if you refocus your efforts? What scares you the most about being generous, and how can you overcome that fear?

I have asked the Lord for one thing; one thing only do I want: to live in the Lord's house all my life, to marvel there at his goodness and to ask his guidance.
Psalm 27:4

8 Don't worry, be happy (Philippians 4:6)

Don't worry, be happy. The song is catchy, and it makes you feel good. But it's really true - the less we worry, the more likely we are to be happy. I'm an A+ worrier. I scored off the charts as a young mom. Was I doing things right? Were the kids growing as they should? What about my older daughter's migraines, which began when she was 18 months old? Was there something serious that we needed to address (thankfully, there wasn't)? What about my younger daughter's hearing loss? How would that impact her growing up? We moved 400 miles to be closer to family. How would we make ends meet? Would my husband's business flourish? What was I going to do? Could I do more? Should I do more?

There were times when I know I faked being happy. I didn't want my girls to see my worries. I might share them with my husband, but really, after a while, those of us who are really good worriers know that others aren't interested in hearing those same worries. Over and over. On replay. My husband is a really patient man (he's married to me, so...), and I could tell when he had had enough of my worrying. Most of the time, I kept the worries in my head and in my heart. How many of the things I worried about came to fruition? Well, not a lot. For those who watch their children drive once they get their licenses, you know how to worry.

Both my girls had accidents. The protection systems in the cars took care of them. I know there are many who have not been so lucky. My anxious heart broke for them in those moments. The things I worried about - the things that some parents have to live with day in and day out - never happened. And I know for some of you, those worries did come to fruition. That's painful, and I do not mean to minimize what happened to your family. I can empathize with your pain and heartache; I can keep you in my prayers and ask for peace. But I can't truly understand what you are feeling. I can only wish for you to find comfort in the days ahead.

On a good day, I took my worries to God. I prayed. I worshiped. I praised. I was thankful. And most of the time, I could step away from those worries. Not always, though. Sometimes I prayed and handed those worries to God; and then kept right on worrying. I've gotten better about this. I can give things to God and let them go. God is good, even when life isn't. There will be things that bring us to our knees; and God will still provide us with what we need in those times. Worrying steals our joy.

As I'm writing this devotional, it's not the best of times in my professional life. Our work lives are a big part of our overall lives. And sometimes, work is just plain awful. It could be the environment, the people, the actual work; it doesn't really matter what the root cause is. We spend so much of our time at work, that we start to think we *are* our work. We're not. And staying in an awful environment, frankly, doesn't honor God. It isn't about how much awfulness we can take before we break. That doesn't honor God. When we are in those types of situations, we aren't our best, either. That doesn't honor God, either. Take courage when you find yourself in a bad work situation. Take your concerns to God. Work through the very real struggles of paychecks and insurance. And listen for God's direction. Sometimes it will be loud; other times you will need to really listen. Do what you need to do for your family, but know that God has a plan for you, and it is not staying where you are not valued.

Prayer: God, we know that You will provide us with what we need. We come to You with a grateful and thankful heart, knowing that You have our best interests in Your heart, and that you will carry our concerns for us. Help us to trust that You will take those worries and give us peace. May we be still and listen for your direction, Lord, in all things. Amen.

Writing: What things do you worry about? How do you address these worries in your prayers? Do you visualize handing your worries over to God? Do you write them down and put them in a prayer jar? What strategies can you try moving forward to let God handle your worries?

Don't worry about anything; instead pray about everything. Tell God what you need, and thank Him for all He has done.
Philippians 4:6

9 God's peace is waiting for you (Philippians 4:7)

I have had an on and off relationship with meditation over the years. I actually enjoy meditation. If I can sit down long enough to do it. I've changed my approach and started listening to my meditation when I walk. Don't worry; I don't close my eyes when I do this. I'm definitely not a graceful person, so that's an injury waiting to happen. If I'm walking, I am listening to something: a meditation, praise music, a podcast. I've found this is a great way for me to reset my thinking in more positive ways. I have found that allowing more positive thoughts into my brain, rather than ruminating on my day, is helpful for me. Give it a try, if you are a fellow ruminator. We should have a support group.

I also have a funny relationship with peace. Funny, strange, not funny, as in comedic. Some days, the peace is just there. I don't have to look for it. I am not anxious. I trust that God has a bigger plan, and I work to listen for His direction in my steps. He'll order them, I know, and I need to be paying attention. Other days, though, the anxiousness follows me like the cloud of dirt follows Pigpen, the Peanuts character. Everywhere I go, that anxiousness is with me. My shoulders are tight. My brain whirs on high. And on those days, I know my reactions are not my best. Notice that I said "reactions," and not "actions and reactions." On my worst days, I don't have actions. That may sound strange, but I feel frozen.

There is much to be said about being in control of your reactions to outside events. We don't have to react negatively when someone cuts us off in traffic. We don't have to chime in when someone is snarky about someone else. We don't have to be offended by anything and everything, though this does seem to be a national pastime at the moment. Why are we offended by what others do? What do their actions matter to us? Why do we lose so much of our peace over their actions and reactions? Even so, I'll challenge you to think about your reactions and interactions with people on a daily basis. A smile to a check out person, allowing someone to go ahead of you in line, and just being a decent human being is important. There have been studies done on this. Our impact goes out four to six levels beyond the person we interacted with. Think about that the next time you feel the need to be unkind to a server in a restaurant or gripe about the price of milk to the check out person.

In Paul's letter to the Philippians, he tells us that God's peace is beyond our understanding. We can try to understand it, but he tells us to keep our hearts and minds in line with Jesus. That's it. You don't need to study peace. You don't need a year-long escape to the Himalayas to find peace. You don't need to ditch your phone (though, personally, I think that helps). For peace, we turn to and lean on God. We don't try to understand how He gives us peace, but we know that He does.

Our prayers are direct lines to Him, and Paul tells us to pray unceasingly. Don't worry. Pray about everything. Tell God what you need. Thank Him for what He has done. Philippians 4:7 is straightforward. Don't worry. Not, pray and then worry. Not tell God what you need and then worry about it. Not thank God and then worry about what is happening in your life. Thank God. Pray. Don't worry. That's it.

Prayer: God, many of us are anxious and afraid, and we are hungering for Your peace. Help us, Lord, to seek You and lay our burdens at Your feet. Teach us to know that when we lean on You, we find peace. Show us how to share that peace with others. Amen.

Writing: Prayer is a key for me to get to peace. Those days when I'm good about doing my devotionals, when I dedicate the time and don't just do them to get them done, when I do guided prayer of some sort, when I meditate…those are the days that are more peaceful. What do you do that helps you find peace? If you are struggling to find peace, what ways are you willing to try to find peace?

And the peace of God, which surpasses all understanding, will guard your hearts and minds through Christ Jesus.
Philippians 4:7

10 Relax, God has a plan (Proverbs 19:21)

What do you want to be when you grow up? We all remember that question from our childhood. Then after high school, where are you going to college? After college, it's what's your plan? You got a job - what's the next promotion? How many of us have heard these phrases? How many of us have *said* these phrases to others? I'm not sure if it is an American thing, but I think it is, a bit. Europeans don't tend to measure their life success by their jobs. They take more holidays, take more time when their children are born...they take more time. Period. What's bigger and better and next - do we really need to get so caught up in that, if we believe what the Bible says in Proverbs 19:21?

Other than wanting to be a horse trainer, which I recognized at a young age was probably not going to be a financially viable option, I always knew I was going to be a teacher. Part of it may have been that growing up in a small town, I didn't know all the options available to me. I knew professional women who were nurses and teachers. Since I got woozy at the sight of blood or serious injury, teaching appealed more. But it was not just that. I loved to learn. I still do. Reading was my way to travel the world, even though it was hard to get out of my zip code. I was able to travel a bit with showing our horses and that was amazing, but my world was pretty small.

My dad didn't go to college; he wasn't able to finish high school due to a serious work injury my grandfather sustained. This was before the days of insurance. Dad needed to go to work to support his family. I'm not sure Dad was all that sad about not finishing high school; it wasn't because he didn't love learning, because he did. But I also remember the wicked sense of humor he had, and the gleam in his eye when he talked about hiding a fishing pole in a tree, then skipping school and riding his bike out to the river to fish. He may not have finished school, but he was one of the wisest men I've known, and it was the breadth of his knowledge and his character that drew people to him. He read something every day. And Dad never met a stranger. He learned from other people. You would have been hard pressed to find someone who didn't like Gordy. He was smart, funny, welcoming, and compassionate.

After dad's injury and his subsequent disability status, he could have been really angry. He could have worried. He could have stressed. And truthfully, he might have been stressed, but he never let on if he was anxious. He still had two kids in school when the explosion caused his injuries; we knew early on that those injuries were a permanent disability. How was he going to provide for his family? I don't know Mom and Dad's thoughts from that time, but I do remember their faith. We went to church. We served at church. And things worked out. Money wasn't plentiful, but it didn't matter. The truth of Proverbs 19:21 was shown in my young life, even if I didn't recognize it at the time.

So why then did I stress (do I stress?) about what's next? God has a plan for each of us. We listen for His word; we try to do His will. And He takes care of the rest. Growing up without a lot of material possessions has impacted my approach to finances. I recognize that I have a scarcity mentality, but recognizing it took well into my adult life. I have enough. More than enough. And I try to do what I can for others (though I am first to admit I don't think I do enough). But more importantly, I *am* enough, in God's eyes. He's got this, and He's going to provide. His plans are good plans. We can rest in that knowledge. I don't need to force His plan; His will is going to be done, in my life, and in yours.

Prayer: Lord, we find it hard to leave our future in Your hands, but we know that You have a plan for us, and that Your will is going to be done. What more could we ask for, Lord, than to have Your hand upon our lives? Thank you for loving us as we are. Amen.

Writing: What do you worry about? Your job? Money? Your family? What's in the future? How can you take steps to trust God and His plan?

People may plan all kinds of things, but the Lord's will is going to be done.
Proverbs 19:21

11 Believe and be steadfast (James 1:6)

Doubts? Who has those? All of us? Well, then, maybe that's part of the problem, eh? We have doubts about our families, our relationships, our work, and we feel like we are stuck in the ocean and being tossed and flipped in every direction. What don't we have doubts on might be an easier question. When I think about that list, it is hard not to be cynical. Something about death and taxes comes to mind.

I've ridden horses for a long time. I have trained horses; I have provided a haven for old horses and worked with a rescue to give them a great home to live out their days. I have ridden horses other people gave up on. As a result, I've been tossed a few times. I always got back in the saddle. That's an adage that has truth in it unless you are injured. There was a time when my belief in my ability to work with and understand horses was in doubt. Nothing had really happened. I'd just been away from them for several years. And I was nervous about getting back in the saddle, literally. This was my own anxiety taking up space in my brain; there wasn't any concrete reason for me to be nervous about riding again, but I was. I've got friends who took nasty falls from their horses, some of whom have the surgery scars and memories to make them leery of a powerful animal with hooves and a tail. And to be honest, respect for horses is a healthy thing. They can very quickly turn into a thousand pounds of uncontrolled power, and if you aren't paying attention. Those who love horses know that managing our doubts, our fears, is a part of being around horses.

There's a term for someone who has no doubts. It's not very flattering. In fact, it's a slam to a person's character. We don't like know-it-alls. We don't like them when we are five, twenty-five, or fifty-five years old. Know-it-alls think they know everything about everything, and really, who can claim that? There's a false idea that having doubts is counterintuitive to being a strong leader. This is absolutely, unequivocally, false. We've all met the person. They are in charge, and they know exactly how everything should be done. They think they are the smartest people in the room and that they know more than everyone else. If we question their ideas, then we become an outlier, a problem, and someone who needs to be removed from the equation, whatever the cost. They do not doubt. They'll drive the bus off the cliff before they will admit that they are wrong. That's not leadership. And here's a thought - that kind of behavior is certainly not Godly.

We don't want to be known as a know-it-all. However, one of the areas where we are told not to doubt is in our conversations with God. In the book of James, we are directed not to doubt our prayers. That means no doubting, ever, to those of you who are still thinking, "yeah, but my prayers haven't come true yet…"

Who hasn't had prayers that didn't come to fruition? Who hasn't prayed for someone's health, for a recovery, for a new job, and had those prayers dashed upon a rock? Who hasn't prayed for deliverance from a bad situation, and then that situation got worse? We all can relate to unanswered prayers, thank you, Garth Brooks, and we all relate to the hurt we feel when the situations we pray about do not end in ways we'd hoped. But doubting God is not the path through this hurt.

And being steadfast in our belief? What's that mean anyway? Steadfast is a centuries-old word with an outdated lexicon. Steadfast is an Old English term, meaning "standing firm," literally, or "place" and "fixed," if you break it down even further. Warriors were steadfast. They stood their ground. They didn't flee. They didn't waver. Steadfast is applicable to this verse; as prayer warriors, we need to stand fast, to not waver, to be resolute in the idea that God hears our prayers. If we doubt, we are not following God's word regarding our prayers, and our anxiousness will increase. Believe that God hears your prayers. Be steadfast in your prayer life.

Prayer: Lord, we know that You hear our prayers, and help us not to doubt that you are working on our behalf, even when we can't see that You are moving. Help us to be steadfast when we pray. We believe that You hear us, and in Your time, You will direct our path in Your way. Help us to remember that it is Your will, and Your timing, Lord. Amen.

Writing: Have you had times when you doubted that God hears your prayers? How did that feel? Did you continue to pray about that issue, or did you give up? Do you think it matters? Moving forward, how might you pray differently, knowing that we must believe and be steadfast in our prayers?

But when you pray, you must believe and not doubt at all. Whoever doubts is like a wave in the sea that is driven and blown about by the wind.
James 1:6

12 Cast all your cares on Him (1 Peter 5:7)

Recently, I heard a great sermon about casting your cares on God. It was part of a series on David and Goliath, and that's a story Christians are familiar with. David, a lowly shepherd boy, the youngest son who has been hanging out in the hills tending his father's sheep while his soldier brothers are fighting for King Saul, is the guy who takes down the giant. David wasn't the star of the team. He wasn't even a trained warrior, and yet, with his slingshot (and God's help), he took down Goliath.

My dad was a depression era baby. So was my mom. Being born in the late 1920s, their childhoods were deeply impacted by the economic crisis of the time. They were thrifty people. They knew how to make a dollar go a long way. They knew fifty uses for that old garden hose, and you didn't throw it out. You might need it. They held on to things, and for good reason. Family photos were treasures. A family heirloom held memories of the people who had passed it down. How blessed am I to still have the Bible that belonged to my great-great-great grandfather? Or my great grandmother's set of china?

I appreciated this aspect of my parents' beliefs, even when I was going through the three-story farmhouse and determining what to keep, what to share, and what to let go. Letting go is hard for all of us, but especially for me. I will admit that. I kept some things at the initial sort that I later let go, either to someone else in the family or to an agency that could pass it on for me. How do we know what to let go of? How do we know we won't need it later? How do we know that things aren't part of our future? How many of us have gotten rid of something, and not a month later, needed that very thing?

Those are easy questions to answer, right? Okay, they aren't easy questions to answer. And we are talking about stuff here and not emotions. Honestly, the emotions and beliefs attached to those tangible things are harder to let go of – the physical items can be released. How do we let go of ideas, of beliefs, that we've held on to but that no longer serve us, and they certainly don't serve God?

If you've ever gone fishing, you know that to cast your line is to let it fly out over the water. You can't grab it tightly. You can't hang on to the reel and slow the progress. Not if you are doing it correctly. You let that line soar, and you let it sail out over the water. That's casting. You let go of the control of the fishing line.

Here's the tough part for you to consider for today. How do you release things that need to go? Anger? Resentment? Fear? How do you release those, cast them, and let God handle them? These things aren't meant to be a part of your future. In that sermon I mentioned above, a key point was that God has a purpose for my life, and I'm not going to get there if I can't let go of the things that I need to release. David let go of many things before he defeated Goliath. His brother's expectations of him (that he was just trying to get attention) and Saul's armor (too big - didn't fit David) are two examples of what David let go before he could move into God's purpose for his life. And David also let go of the stone in the sling. He swung the sling, cast the stone, and let it soar and complete God's purpose. The giant was defeated by letting go and trusting God. We are called to do the same.

Prayer: Heavenly Father, we try too hard to do things on our own, and that means that we don't share our burdens with You when we should. Help us to give up control, to cast our cares to You, Lord. Help us to release these concerns and not hold on to them. Help us to trust that You will carry us through. Amen.

Writing: How well do you cast your cares to God? Do you throw them His way, but still hang on to them? If you are good at casting your concerns and forgetting about them, what helps you to do that? Take some time and write out your cares and concerns. End this journaling time with writing this verse at the end. Truly cast those cares to Him and see what happens!

God cares for you, so turn all your worries to Him.
1 Peter 5:7

13 Doing good is good (Proverbs 14:22)

We are hard on ourselves; often much harder than we are on others. Our self-talk is often harsh and unkind. We'd never think of talking to one of our friends or family the way that we talk to ourselves. Why is that? Why are we so insecure about our own value and worth? We often have trouble of thinking of ourselves as being good, just the way God made us. Proverbs 14:22 reminds us that we need to do good. We are God's creation and God's handiwork. We are inherently good. But do we really see ourselves that way? And when we don't, does that make it harder for us to do good?

I'm tallish for our family. I'm not really that tall (5'7"), but only a couple female cousins are taller. Many are smaller, 5 foot 3 inches and under, and while I liked having my "height" on the basketball court, I didn't love being asked to get things off shelves. When I worked in a cubicle farm at an engineering company, I could see over the partitions. No one else in my all-female group could do that. I was asked to get things down off shelves there, too. My middle-of-the-road height was kind of annoying. I wasn't willowy; I was curvy. I'm even curvier now. I enjoy physical activity, and I'm outside a lot when the weather is decent. But I'm not where I'd like to be, health-wise. Many things factor into that, all of which I'm working on, but that's the reality. And I can be brutal when talking to myself about where I am and where I need to be.

Often our negative self-talk is around our appearance, or our flaws, or our mistakes. God sees our heart. He doesn't care about our weight, or our hair style, or our clothing choices. He doesn't care if we've made mistakes. There's only one perfect being, and it isn't me, and it isn't you. So why do we act like we must be perfect in order for God to love us? The good news is He loves us anyway. Flaws and all. In spite of our mistakes. God made us. God loves us. And He has plans for us to do good while we are here on this earth.

God didn't just create us so we can do whatever we want. We are created in Christ to do good works, and God knows His plan for us. The hard part can be staying still enough to hear what He wants us to do. I know I've heard that small voice sometimes when it tells me to step up and help someone; I try to do the right thing in those moments. I have a hard time not helping others. I have difficulty not giving people money when they need it, when I have been so blessed. Yes, I have been taken advantage of. And that's okay. God doesn't tell us to do good things and to attach strings to those good things. He just tells us to do good things. No strings. No expectations of recognition. No expectations of reward. No expectations that someone will do something good for us. That can become difficult, especially if you have had several bad experiences. But I encourage you to do good anyway. God expects it.

Prayer: Heavenly Father, we thank You for the love You freely give us, and for the blessings You have showered upon us. Give us a servant heart to help others and share Your love in our corner of the world. Remind us that we are loved by You, as we are, and that we can show that love to others by giving freely of our time and talents. Amen.

Writing: Do you struggle with helping others? What are some ways that you try to show God's love to others through good works? While we know that good works do not get us into heaven, Christians are expected to be servants. What small voice have you heard telling you to help others? Have you listened to that voice? Will you in the future?

You will earn the respect and trust of others if you work for good ... Proverbs 14:22

14 Doing what is right, is right (Romans 12:17)

It is awesome if you are reading this devotional and you've never been hurt. That would be an amazing gift. Unfortunately, most have been hurt by others, and sometimes those others are the people who are supposed to care for us, love us, unconditionally. And for some people, they've been harmed by evil. We don't like to talk about that much, that there is true evil in the world, but it is true. Romans 12:17 is a comfort, and the verses after it assure us that God will handle those who do wrong. Even so, there are times when we'd really, *really*, like to do wrong to someone who has hurt us. That's our human-ness. That's our fallibility. God knows that our nature is to want to react, to make that person (or persons) feel hurt like we did. He assures us that we need to let it go and let Him handle it. This isn't a suggestion. Jesus tells us to forgive because our Father forgave us.

That doesn't mean that all things can be forgiven. We read about and hear about awful things that happen. Sometimes it is within families. Sometimes it is random. Sometimes it is planned evil-doing. And still, we are called to do good to these people. I've read countless stories where a victim has forgiven the person who harmed them. These individuals are heroes to me. After everything they went through, all of the pain and heartache, they can still find it in their hearts to forgive. That's an amazing portrait of faith and forgiveness. Forgiveness doesn't mean that what happened was acceptable; forgiveness is letting God have our hurt and leaving the rest to Him to handle.

What does doing good to those who've done us wrong even look like? My husband is better at this than I am. He sets a great example for me. "Let it go," he'll say. Or my favorite (you should read that with the sarcasm with which is intended), "Be the bigger person." The Irish part of me wants to hang on to that hurt, the grievance, the offense, or the anger. But that doesn't help me, and I'm learning that my husband is right in his ability to move past wrongs as quickly as possible. To be clear, I have no problem with doing good works. I look for opportunities every day. My catch is when someone has hurt me, intentionally or unintentionally, and then God asks me to do good to that particular person, I have to really, really engage with prayer. At best, I want to ignore or avoid them. I'd be happy to not ever run into them again or even think about them again. I don't ever wish someone harm; truly, I don't. But I have to work really hard to want to do good for them. I will need to keep working on this, I know.

Families are a great example of people who should love each other unconditionally, but that is not always the case. Money is often the root of evil, and when money is involved, the worst can come out in family members. We all know someone who has become estranged from a family member due to an inheritance or other financial venture. I know several. Unfortunately, I know this pain personally as well. The pain in these stories is real. How can people let money be more important than their siblings, children, etc.? God recognizes that pain, and He wants us to continue to do good, even when others have done wrong. That doesn't necessarily mean reconciling a relationship, but it does mean forgiveness. It does mean not repaying wrong with a wrong. It means doing good.

Prayer: Lord, help me to understand that when someone is not good to me, I can still be good to them. You know our hurt and fears, Lord, and You alone will be the judge of our actions. Help us to be a light in a world that has too much darkness. Amen.

Writing: What situations do you think of where you've been hurt by someone, and yet are challenged to do good? How can you move towards goodness in this situation? How can you be a symbol of God's light and love? How does forgiveness and reconciliation factor into this situation? Have you forgiven the person? Reconciliation is not always possible; write your thoughts about what reconciliation may or may not look like in this situation.

Do not repay anyone evil for evil. Be careful to do what is right in the eyes of everyone. Romans 12:17

15 Be still - remember? (Deuteronomy 3:22)

This is about the halfway point of this devotional. Congratulations on making it this far! Let's go back to the original idea of this study. Be still. How are you doing on that? We've all heard the adages. If you don't stand up for yourself, who will? If you don't look out for number one, you'll step in number two. Attack first, or you'll be attacked. All of these sayings revolve around one tenet - that we should look out for ourselves first. Deuteronomy 3:22 helps us understand that the fight does not belong to us.

I'm a little sister. Those who are little sisters know what that means. We're a feisty bunch. We often had to shoulder our way into the conversation, to get to the biscuits, or to be heard. We are determined, and we won't be ignored. Being still and not standing up for myself - that's counterintuitive to my birth-order position as a little sister. Later in life, I thought that if I tried hard enough to tell my side of the story, to fight my battles on my own, that I could be successful. I know now that even if I did win some battles, it wasn't because of my will or my strength.

Sometimes we confuse being still with not doing anything, and we should probably talk about that. Being still and trusting God doesn't mean we are stagnant. It doesn't mean that we sit meekly and wait for what comes next. It doesn't mean that we do nothing during this time of being still. What can we do while we wait on God? We can take a step of faith. We can serve others in our community. We can read the Bible or participate in a Bible study. We can watch for opportunities that God is sending us and be prepared to act when we recognize those opportunities. Being still is making sure that we don't get in God's way by acting in ways that don't honor Him.

God wants to fight for us. I wonder how many times I got in His way trying to fight for myself? There have been many instances over the years where I gave my battles over to Him. I was tired. I didn't have the energy to continue, and so I gave Him my battles. Those who know me know that I will not shy away from a tough conversation or an uncomfortable situation. Most of the time, these conversations went fine and the situations were resolved. Uncomfortable situations happen to all of us, and like most everyone, there were times when I didn't know how to approach the conflict. I asked God to lead, and I worked on being still. God will show up for you in those situations. He has, repeatedly, for me.

Even so, it can be hard to be still when we are afraid. When the enemy attacks us, we can instinctively come out swinging. Fear often makes us take an action, that in hindsight, we probably shouldn't have taken. The fight or flight instinct is strong. There's also a freeze instinct, where you don't act at all when under attack, but that isn't what we're talking about here. Being still is making a choice to stand firm on the solid rock and letting God fight our battles for us. And for those battles that cannot be avoided, He will guide us. I know there is scripture about putting on the armor of God, but we'll talk about that another day in another journal. For now, let's focus on being still, doing what we can, listening for His voice, and getting out of His way.

Prayer: Lord, help me to understand that I don't have to do everything on my own. I trust You Lord to fight my battles. I will be still and wait on You. Help me to hear Your voice in the stillness and to listen for Your direction. Amen.

Writing: Are you able to be still and let God fight your battles? If so, what is your approach? If not, why do you think that is? If you struggle with letting go, what can you do in the future to change your mindset? For those times when you can't avoid the battle, how can you move forward with God's help?

Do not be afraid of them; the Lord your God himself will fight for you. Deuteronomy 3:22

16 I will trust in Him (Isaiah 12:2)

Today was one of those days at work. Some of you may have had one, too. You know, the day that starts by you starting your coffee, but forgetting to put a cup under the drippy thing? The day that starts with a text from your boss before 7 am, that there's a problem at work and you need to fix it. Now. Then you end up having to call most of your team before 7 am as well, to get the problem resolved before everyone gets to work. Then that same day ends with work drama causing real hurt and pain to several people, and you're not in a position to fix it, and those who can, well, they won't. In this case, they supported those instigating the drama, which only made the situation worse.

I will admit, I'm not always at my best, and though I'm a morning person, starting my day this way can be hard. Ending my day with drama is about the worst thing for me because I will ruminate about it for hours. I have been fortunate to work with mostly great people, and they always step up and get things done. But, sometimes, people are just not my favorite. I know they are God's creations. I know I should be more patient. But some days, I struggle. If this resonates with you, I'm glad not to be alone. If it doesn't, then good for you. I'm glad you have healthy ways of dealing with those stresses.

God made us all different, and we all handle things in our unique ways. It's easy to say that everyone else's approach is wrong, and yours is right. We all know that isn't true. And not everyone in the world is out to make us miserable on a given day. But, there are things that happen in our lives that aren't what God wants to see. Coworkers are mean-spirited, spiteful, and angry at the world. We might end up being targets of those feelings. Most days, we can respond in healthier ways, knowing that these negative actions don't need to impact us, that the person's issues really aren't about us.

But other days, it is hard. We get worn down. We become exhausted. And spending time around negative influences, day in and day out, is just not good for most of us. I do what I can to spend more time with positive people, those who are inherently good humans (and yes, even they can have a bad day). But most of us don't have a way to isolate ourselves from people who, frankly, we'd just rather not deal with. I'm sure their families love them. I'm sure God loves them. But I'd rather be in another county than have to deal with them.

The days when I'm in a better place, I recognize that I don't have to have it all together on my own. As we know in Isaiah 12:2, we can rely on God's power and strength, on His grace, to do better. He can give me the confidence to respond in better ways, and I can lean on His grace when I fall down. In my heart, I know better than to let other people control my responses to situations. But the reality is, sometimes things happen that tip us over or get us off center. We can lean into God, trust Him, and use His power and strength to do the best we can. We can trust that He is in our corner, and we can trust Him to see us through those hard times.

Prayer: Lord, thank You for watching over us and protecting us. When we face hard times in our lives, Lord, help us remember that we can trust in You. Remind us that You are our shield and our fortress, and that we stand on the solid rock. Help us to be kind in our reactions and responses. Amen.

Writing: How do you react to unkind people? Are there times in your work or home life where you are beat down and discouraged? How can going to the Lord help you through these times? How can you call on His help? If you've had an experience that's bothering you, write about it here, and ask for God's help in working through that situation.

God is my savior; I will trust Him and not be afraid. The Lord gives me power and strength; He is my savior.
Isaiah 12:2

17 Joy will be coming (Psalm 126:5)

"I've got the joy, joy, joy, joy, down in my heart..." Admit it - you sang that sentence in your head. If you sang this song in Sunday School, you might have even done some hand motions to go along with it. We feel joy when we are connected to God. But joy can be elusive if we are struggling. At my darkest, I wondered if I would feel anything again. Anger. Excitement. Happiness. Joy? That seemed so far-fetched that I didn't even hope for joy. I can remember winding down in bed one night, watching late night TV, and listening to the laughter during the monologue. I literally wasn't able to laugh at the jokes. I'm not sure I could muster a smile. I realized that night, I had lost my joy. And honestly, I was afraid I might never get it back. It was a dark time.

Midwesterners are known for being nice. You've seen the comedians poke fun at us, and it's painfully accurate. We will be nice, but the joke is that we are really just being passive aggressive. Midwesterners often minimize how we are feeling. We may not express feelings at all, actually. If we do get to the point where the emotional dam breaks, those emotions are likely to come out in a flood. We're quite good at that. Holding everything in until the dam bursts, and then the flood, a slew of feelings let out all at once, rushes over everyone and everything in our path.

Midwesterners are also really good at playing the "at least" card. Well, I am feeling down, but you know, my friend has it worse, or at least I have my health, or at least I have a job, so I can't complain. I'm not sure where this comes from, the thought that we aren't as bad off as someone else, so we should feel better about how things are going for us. Sometimes, life is hard. Whether it is a big or small problem - it doesn't matter. Your feelings are your feelings. Acknowledge them. Work through them. Move past them. But don't ignore them. That won't help at all. Flooding is a well-known psychological phenomenon; the aftermath of those episodes are not helpful to you or to those around you. Flooding – letting all of our pent-up emotions through the flood gates – is harmful for us and to those around us.

Our sadness is not a bad thing. When we feel deeply, those feelings are shown, sometimes in tears. Sometimes in oceans of tears. But God helps us remember that our tears will reap joy. We keep our eyes on Jesus, we cry those tears, and we reap the joy. I did eventually find my joy again. My laughter has even made an appearance. I thank God for these words to give us light when we are lost in darkness. After every storm, there is sunshine again. Sometimes it takes us more time than we'd like to travel through that storm, but God's promises are there through it all. Joy will come in the morning.

Prayer: Lord, thank You for helping us acknowledge our sadness. You keep our tears in a bottle, Lord, and You know how our hearts ache. When we are in hard seasons, help us to know that the joy will be coming. Help us to keep our focus on You, and to know that these storms will pass, and our joy can be found in Your promises. Amen.

Writing: Have you ever lost your joy, or felt such deep sadness that you couldn't laugh? Write about those times here, and if you are still in that season, ask God to hear your prayer for joy.

Those who sow in tears shall reap in joy.

Psalm 126:5

18 Let God fight your battles (Deuteronomy 20:4)

One of my favorite worship songs is "See a Victory" by Elevation Worship, which relates to this verse in Deuteronomy, though much of the lyrics are based on a different verse in Corinthians. Worship music has always been important to me. I've sang in praise teams, sang for weddings, sang for fun.... God's word set to music is worship for me. This verse reminds us that weapons are going to be formed against us, things go on in the dark to conspire against us. But we don't have to worry. God is fighting for us. God will win. There's no question in the outcome.

None of us like to think we have enemies, but the reality is harsher. Sometimes, those people who are hard to be around are the ones trying to bring us down. Sometimes, people are fighting their own demons, but we are caught in the backlash of their actions and emotions. We can be intentionally or unintentionally harmed. God and His angel armies are fighting for us. We don't see them, but I am encouraged by knowing they are there. I like to think that my ancestors, those who have gone before me, and without whom I wouldn't be here, are somehow angels for me, too. I am pretty sure someone who reads this is going to say that doesn't have a Biblical basis. They'd likely be right. But God also talks about how we will be blessed for generations upon generations if we worship God and follow His commands.

As the family genealogist, I feel a deep, abiding connection to my relatives that I've never known. As I research their stories, their lives, finding puzzle pieces about their journeys through life, I am struck by how many times I find something that is familiar. I wasn't there. I didn't know them. And yet, I feel like I do. My great-great-great grandfather, Heinrich Frederick Christian Grupe (Henry) was a German Lutheran pastor in the late 1800s. After emigrating from Germany in his early teens, he went to seminary in St. Louis, and then travelled throughout the Midwest, setting up churches in the wilderness, preaching in German. His Bible and his Heidelberg Catechism are in my glass cabinet in my living room. Both books are in German, and yet, when I open those tomes, I am connected to him, the words make sense, even in another language.

I can't explain that connection. I can't explain that when I map out the photos I have, and I have several photos of him, I can gather a sense of who he was: an austere, focused, God-fearing, purposeful man. How can I get a sense of this man so clearly? How can we get a sense of people, especially family members, whom we never met? We can read the stories and the facts about them; but we know them better than we know strangers. Their lives are part of our present, just as our lives will be part of our descendants' reality someday.

I have always been fascinated by God's archangels: Michael, Gabriel, Raphael, and Uriel. These super angels are the original avengers. Wouldn't we all want one of them watching over us? There are so many Christians, and only four of them. What do these angel armies watching over us look like? Mine would be medieval knights, riding impressive warhorses, if I get to imagine them. Chivalrous, honorable knights who are ensuring that good prevails in God's name. These archangels are fighting God's battles 24/7.

It brings peace to think about God being on our side, of fighting against our enemies. Fighting is hard; it is exhausting. Trying to defend ourselves, to ward off the enemy, to stave off evil...we can't do it by ourselves. And God isn't just fighting for us. He will bring us into victory. This verse is clear. God just won't be with us during the fight. He will win the fight. We will see a victory through Him.

Prayer: Lord, send Your armies to protect us from the enemy. Watch over our family and friends; be with those who need Your protection. Remind us, Lord, that we can rely on You and that we aren't fighting the enemy alone. Give us Your peace. Help us rest knowing that You are fighting our battles. Amen.

Writing: What are your thoughts about God fighting your battles? Do you see that as being true for you? If not, what holds back your belief? Has something happened that seems to be counter to this idea? If His angel armies are watching over you, can you visualize what they look like? Describe them? What does victory look like to you? If God will ensure that we have that victory, how does this impact your beliefs for the future in difficult times?

The Lord your God is going with you, and He will give you victory. Deut. 20:4

19 Better hang on: good things ahead (Isaiah 43:19)

Sometimes we get really bogged down in our day-to-day lives. It is especially hard to look ahead when things are not going well. So what's your plan? What are you going to do next? What are you going to achieve? When's your next trip? What's your New Year's resolution? How many of us are driven by these questions? We accomplish something; we immediately move on to what we are we going to accomplish next. Granted, completing tasks and projects feels good. And getting a promotion, or a raise, or a new job, feels good. But there's nothing in the Bible that talks about us needing to achieve, to climb whatever ladder we are climbing, and there is certainly nothing about doing better and better in our careers. How do we balance that? The need to feel like we have a purpose, and to feel like we are purposeful, is a strong human need. Where does it come from? How do we feed it in ways that honor God?

I was traveling for work earlier this year and flipping through the channels at the end of the day. I came across a pastor speaking about purpose. She was speaking about setting goals and about prayer. But her take was different. She was talking about our tendency to pray small prayers. Yikes, that took hold. I'm not sure why, but I'm reticent about asking God for big things. Maybe because some of the mountains I've asked Him to move still stand tall? Those mountains will be moved in His time, and for His will, but am I a little miffed that His will and my will don't line up? Yes, I am, as a matter of fact, but that's my human-ness.

Or is the issue deeper than that? Do I pray small prayers because I feel like I don't deserve those big things? If we listen to the negative voices in our environment, we may think this, that we don't deserve big blessings from God. God has big things in store for us; but those things may not be exactly what we are thinking about achieving. This takes us back to the concept of being still or asking God for direction and being still enough to listen, really listen, to what He's trying to tell us. We can't know God's will, and we can't even try to discern how our lives will ultimately play out. Even so, we don't need to pray small prayers.

Isaiah 43:19 tells us that God's plan is bigger than we can imagine. God can and will do big things in our lives. Sometimes we ask for them; sometimes they are gifts. But to think that we can somehow control what God is going to do in our lives; that's where we can get sideways. Pray those big prayers. Dream big dreams. Take the steps that you can to achieve the dreams God has put into your heart. And along the way, trust in God's timing and in His will for our lives. Sometimes, dreams don't come to fruition. Other times, things we couldn't possibly have dreamed about come into our lives, and we are doubly blessed. And there are also times when we are down and discouraged because our lives just don't seem to be playing out the way we had hoped. That's when we need to remind ourselves that God will make a way for us, He will lead us on the right paths, and He will bring us through. Always. That we can count on.

Prayer: Lord, am I guilty of asking too little of You? Am I not listening to Your direction for my life? I know that You have placed dreams in my heart, and I trust that You will provide what I need when I need it. You will provide the path for me; I need to be prepared to listen and to act. Amen.

116

Writing: What would you pray for, if you could pray for anything and have it come true? What do you currently pray for? Do you pray for yourself? For others? What do you think shapes your prayers? Do you see a pattern?

Look, I am about to do something new; even now it is coming. Do you not see it? Indeed, I will make a way in the wilderness; paths in the desert.
Isaiah 43:19

20 When we are under attack, look up (Psalm 59:1)

The movie *Mean Girls* is the quintessential teenage flick. A new girl moves into town, wants to join up with the popular group, lies a bit, is found out as an imposter, and then is mercilessly attacked. Mayhem ensues. The bullied girl wins in the end. The bullies are put in their place. All good, right? Good triumphs in the end.

Fast forward a few years to the workplace. Most good fiction mimics real life, unfortunately. Some of these bullies haven't grown up at all. *Harvard Business Review* has written about mean girls in the workplace. Research studies are conducted about the impacts of negative women on other women (and men). These aren't teenage bullies. They are grown women who attack their colleagues, primarily, and often to disastrous personal and professional results. The bullied employee doesn't win (or rarely wins), and there is often significant fallout from these attacks. Losses abound, in relationships, in careers, and in opportunities. No one wins in these situations, even if the bully does succeed in their attempts to harm someone. There are efforts to strengthen employees' rights in the workplace against bullies. Several states have introduced legislation. We have to have laws to protect us from adult bullies; let that sink in.

Some of us have been attacked, been lied about, had rumors spread about us, and otherwise been bullied. It is hard to defend yourself against these shadow attacks. People will believe what they want to believe; it is virtually impossible to get ahead of the lies. Bullies will create a false narrative about you that isn't true and spread untruths and revel in spreading innuendos. Some people take great joy in harming others, though they often protest that they would never do such a thing. Actions speak much louder than words. Some of the meanest, angriest people I've ever met...have sat in a church pew, professed publicly to be a Christian, or had a Bible verse in their email signature. And they've been the first one to believe rumors, spread rumors, and harm others. That is hard to comprehend.

Younger me tried to defend myself against these attacks. I've also stood up for other people who were attacked (and will continue to do so). When I didn't know better, when I was being attacked, I tried harder for people to like me. I tried to change any little flaw I had. And I was hard on myself; harder than any boss or mentor ever was. Maybe you've had those situations, too. Life isn't fair, things get sideways, and you find yourself trying to defend your actions, your position, and the space that you take up and air that you breathe. Older me has realized that nothing I could have said or done in those situations would have changed the hearts and minds of those people. They had decided they were right in their perceptions of me, and whatever actions they took against me, even the bullying, was justified.

Now, I know that I am safe from my enemies. If I need to leave a situation, God has my back. If I need to walk away, things will be okay. And maybe most importantly, God is there to hear our hurts, take our pain, and give us hope. Our enemies are still there. They can still hurt us. But He will bring us through those trials, and He will protect us.

Looking back, I also know that there were times when I was not kind, or supportive, or understanding. I could have done better; I could have been more honest about why certain actions were being undertaken, as an example, but my intuition tells me the outcome, that someone was hurt, may not have changed. There are times in our lives that we'd like to replay, to do over, so that we could make different choices. We can pray about those times, too, and ask God to help us repair what we can repair, and to bring peace to anyone whom we may have harmed.

Prayer: Jesus, thank you for protecting me from my enemies. The devil roars like a lion and seeks to destroy, but You, our God, protect us. Help us to know our worth to You and to understand when to walk away from those who seek to harm us. Keep us rooted in grace, Lord, and to take care that our actions do not harm others. Amen.

Writing: Have you ever been bullied? Conversely, have you ever harmed someone? Have you ever stood by and watched someone be bullied and not done anything? Take time to be honest about this. How did you feel in those situations? How could you take your fears and hurts to God in this time? What can you do differently the next time you are in a situation where you or someone else is being bullied?

Rescue me from my enemies, my God; protect me from those who rise up against me.
Psalm 59:1

21 Looking good, inside and out (1 Samuel 16:7)

We are a culture obsessed with looking good, on the outside. Over the last 20 years, we've become more concerned about the inside, too, but probably more for health reasons than for spiritual reasons. Our obsessions with appearances, in particular, can really get in our way. This self-centeredness can be detrimental to our relationships with others. We are so focused on ourselves, that we literally can't see others, or we can't empathize with what others are feeling or going through.

While we know life isn't fair, it doesn't make it less difficult when something happens to shake us. The rise in bad behavior in the past 10 years has been telling in American society. The impact of reality television is telling. Don't like someone? Go after them. Someone harm you? Cut them out of your life. Our political parties can't get along. Families can't get along. Friends ghost you after 20 years of friendship. Tolerance for differences has declined. Intolerance of anyone who isn't like us has increased. Hate crimes are on the rise, and as of this writing, there are two major wars going on in the world. Something is broken.

It isn't wrong to want to feel good and look good. Most of us want to be healthy, physically. We also want to feel good about ourselves. What is the disconnect between wanting God's love for ourselves and showing God's love to others? Some might say our inability to truly love ourselves, as we are, is a major factor. We are uber focused on our physical body, and if that isn't looking the way we want it too, everything else can be at risk. Broken relationships are hurtful; hurt people hurt other people. The question for me is, why don't people take their hurts to Jesus, rather than taking them out on their friends, family, and coworkers? Why do we use our hurts to lash out at others?

Difficult conversations are just that - difficult - but really, if most people had a conversation, many things could be worked out. What I've found, though, is people would rather dig in, continue to say hurtful things, and destroy friends and colleagues. I don't know why. It is a disappointing and unGodly development. Most of the people I know who have done these things? They are sitting in the church pew on Sunday. They are professing how they are doing what's best for themselves. And my very favorite, they even tell you they prayed about it, and that's why they are choosing a particular course of action, even though there is chaos happening all around them. It is hard not to be judgmental in these situations, even though we know God doesn't want us to judge them. We know we need to leave that to Him, but it is hard!

We can fool ourselves into thinking that any action we undertake that hurts someone else is warranted. But God knows our hearts. If you've ever been the victim of gossip, you know how hard it is not to defend yourself. What I've learned is that people who want to believe the worst in you, will do so, no matter what you say or do to prove them wrong. The converse is true as well. People who know you, really know you, and nothing someone says will change their opinion of your value. Relying on the human condition and people to validate your worth is a losing proposition. 1 Samuel 16:7 tells us to focus on how God sees us. He sees our heart, and he knows the truth. Let the haters hate, right? God knows the truth. Take your hurt to him and let His love be enough. Keep working on your wholeness, inside and out. But remember that the mirror is not your gauge. God's understanding of who we are is the accurate measure.

Prayer: Lord, help us to be honest with ourselves. Help us to love ourselves enough that we don't feel the need to hurt others. Help us to be aware of our actions, our intent, and our impact on those around us. Remind us, God, that what matters is how You see us. Amen.

Writing: Looking into our own hearts can be scary. Sometimes we stay busy so we don't stop and think about our actions. What about you? What's in your heart? Write about a time where you aren't proud of what you did and try to work through the why. What was going on at that time? How did lashing out at others impact you? Conversely, write about a time when you were proud of something you did or said. How did you pause and recenter before speaking and acting? Was prayer a part of the equation?

The LORD doesn't see things the way you see them. People judge by outward appearance, but the Lord looks at the heart.
1 SAMUEL 16:7

22 Holding on to hope (Hebrews 10:23)

Christians are a hopeful people. The critics will say that hope is not a strategy; well, that may be true, but I would qualify that without hope, there is no strategy. Hope is one of the big three of the Christian theology (faith, hope, and love). Hope is what we have at the end of the day, especially after a particularly tough day. Hope is there in the morning when we rise to greet the day's challenges. We hope because we know God, and we know He has a plan for us. Sometimes, waiting on that plan or stepping into that plan, can be frustrating. I get it.

Hope in the face of adversity gives us strength. And sometimes, things are really dark during that time of struggle. Last fall, a young friend, a father of three, who had just announced with his wife they were expecting their fourth child, lost his life in a farm accident. There are no platitudes that can ease the pain of his wife, his family, or his friends. It wasn't his time to go. That's the cruelty of accidents. One minute, you are there, and the next minute, you are gone. Those left behind are crushed under the sadness, the uncertainty, and the disbelief. We know that the person who has left us is now in Heaven, but we're still here, and we are grieving. I'd known Mitch for 20 years, and he'd married a local girl. Everyone who knew Mitch, loved him. He quite literally lit up a room when he walked in. And in the blink of an eye, he was gone. No one on earth can understand why.

And yet, we hope. We hope that people won't forget him. We hope that people will be kinder to each other, because Mitch, at his core, was kindness personified. We hope that his wife and children will find their way, find peace, find love, and find acceptance in the years ahead. God's love for us doesn't promise that we won't hurt, that we won't be sad, that we won't understand why something has happened. He loves us through these things, and our faith will see us through the hard times. Hebrews 10:23 tells us to stay faithful, and to hold on unswervingly to the hope we say that we have. I know there are times that have been unsteady, that have derailed us, but God reminds us that He is faithful, through it all. We can place our hope in Him.

Please know that in no way am I minimizing the hurt, the devastation, the grief, or the other emotions we have when an incident like this happens. Yes, we have hope in God, and we know that our faith will see us through. But those emotions we feel are real, and our ability to process them and move through our grief will be individual and profound. What happens for one person in a year, might not happen for another person for five or ten years. The small town I live in has had too many accidents, too many young people, who have been taken too soon. Our empathy, our understanding, and our support for each other in these times is paramount. We can't know what another is going through, but we can sit beside our friends and family, we can be present, and we can pray.

In "Heaven Changes Everything," Big Daddy Weave talks about hope at length. The backstory of this song is that the main singer loses his younger brother at a young age. If we didn't have hope in heaven, if we didn't know that our home is not on Earth, if we didn't realize that God makes all things right, in His time, our journey would be for nothing. Eternity changes everything for Christians. We know that we will someday find beauty beyond the pain, that we'll someday be reunited in Heaven. That's the hope we cherish and hold close.

Prayer: Father, be close to those who are hurting and tired. Be with them, comfort them, in their time of sadness. Help them, Lord, to know that you are near, and that the promise of a brighter tomorrow is ahead. Help us to hope in the future and in Your promises. Amen.

Writing: If you've lost a loved one, and you want to write a memorial to that person here, use the space for that. It is often said that the best memorial to someone is to live a life embodying their very best traits. What would that look like for you? How does hope factor into wanting to be our best while in this world?

Let us hold unswervingly to the hope we profess, for He who promised is faithful.
Hebrews 10:23

23 We are never alone (Psalm 16:8)

During the pandemic, our worldview changed. For some of us, this was a dramatic and unwelcome change. For others, the shift was a welcome one. We saw people react in a broadly diverse range of ways. Some did what they could to protect themselves and others; others did not. Some reveled in the shift in work culture; others did not. Some couldn't wait to get back to work, to the office, to the commute. Others....you get the picture.

During the pandemic and the subsequent shutdown, some of us had more time to be creative. We had more time for our hobbies. We took time to reach out to friends who lived far away. We had Friday night Zoom calls to gather and laugh. We took walks, we slowed down, and we spent more time with people in our bubble. I found more time than ever to read and think. Those who know me, know that if I have more time to read, I am in my happy place.

But for others, the shutdown brought loneliness and uncertainty. Not everyone enjoyed the alone time. For some, it was not a good time at all. They were lonely. They were afraid. They were uncertain. They were angry about how things had changed. I might have been a little angry the first few days for a very selfish reason; the NCAA basketball tournaments were cancelled that year. I look forward to those games every year!

There were no spring sports, no school, no proms, and no graduations. Weddings, family reunions, travel plans; events were put on hold. It was unlike anything we'd ever seen.

Churches closed their doors. Some moved their services online. Some had a hard time surviving. Christians had to shift in how we praised, worshipped, and gathered. For some, this impacted their faith in negative ways. How can you practice your faith without the cultural structures in place, without going to the building?

Psalm 16:8 reminds us that even in drastic events, like the pandemic, God is with us. He walks before us, beside us, and behind us. He knows what our future holds because He is creating it. We can take comfort in that thought. He is right beside me. He is right beside you. And we do not need to be shaken. We do not need to fear what is coming next.

I really hope that we don't have another pandemic in my lifetime, but the reality is, I don't know that for certain. Seems like every century, humans need to be reminded about historical events that alter our world in significant ways. In fact, we might as well expect that something will indeed happen to shake us. The good news is that God is there with us. In the hard times, in the unknown times, and in the good times. He's there, and He's waiting for us to remember that.

Prayer: Father, thank You for always being with us. You are with me, in good times, in bad times, and in uncertain times. You know what is ahead for me, and Your goodness and mercy will follow me, all the days of my life. I can stand firm in that knowledge and worship You for Your presence in my life. Amen.

 **Writing:** Has there been a time when you felt alone? Write about that time, and how you felt God's nearness at that time. If you didn't feel His presence, be honest about that. Also consider your part in that time; did you talk with God or shut Him out? How was your prayer life? If that time comes upon you again where you feel alone or isolated, what would you do again? What would you do differently?

I know the Lord is always with me. I will not be shaken, for He is right beside me.
Psalm 16:8

_____

_____

_____

_____

_____

_____

_____

_____

_____

_____

_____

_____

_____

24 Pray for who? Seriously? (Matthew 5:44)

It is easy to pray for people we love. It is easy to pray for people we like. It is easy to pray for people we don't know, but with whom we have a common friend or family member. We can bow our heads and send prayers around the world to those who are suffering in a war or from a tragedy. But pray for our enemies? Pray for those who make our lives miserable? Really, Lord? Isn't that asking a lot?

I have a friend who is really good at praying for people she doesn't like. She's also challenged me to do the same. Why do I withhold prayers for people who have hurt me? What good does that do? How does that honor God? I do still like this friend, by the way. She's the best sort of friend: she loves me but she also challenges me to do better. I can get as singularly focused as the next person, and not in a good way. When I'm hurt, I work hard not to push that hurt on to someone else. And yet, I know that sometimes I fail in this respect.

We all can think of someone who has hurt us. Too often, those who have hurt us are those we are most close to. And many times, those people are no longer in our lives, but we still think of them often. That could be a sign for us; if we are still thinking about the hurt, the anger, or the incident, we likely need to be praying for the other people involved. We should even be praying for those we don't like or for those who may have harmed us. Forgiveness is our part; God will take care of the rest. Reconciliation may not be possible, but praying for others puts the scales in God's hands, where they belong. We don't get to decide how those hurts are reconciled or if the relationships can be saved. But we can pray. God expects it of us.

What do those prayers look like? Do an Internet search and you'll find literally hundreds of ideas for how to pray for those who've hurt or harmed you. There are prayers for those who have persecuted you. There are prayers to love your enemies, prayers to destroy enemies, prayers for protection against your enemies, and even prayers of vengeance. I was quite surprised by the number of angry prayers that I found, actually. I'm not seeing those options as good ones for me. You'll have to decide your prayer path based on your values. Those scales of justice I mentioned? They are not in my hands; judge not, right? It is definitely not easy!

In Matthew 5:44, God directs us to love our enemies. That's a tall order, but He doesn't give us the easy way out, and I'm thankful for that. Making peace with our enemies may mean praying that the hurt and anger go away, so that you no longer ruminate on what happened. Making peace may mean actual reconciliation with the person. It also may mean that you do not reconcile. Making peace may mean giving those hurts over to God and letting go of them. Really letting go of those hurts. Not dragging them around with us every day, letting them steal our joy. Praying for those who persecuted us takes time and careful thought. God doesn't give us a pass and tell us to avoid prayers we don't like. He is very specific in His direction to love our enemies and to pray for them. This may take me a lifetime to get right.

Prayer: Lord, thank You for giving us the Holy Spirit, who can work through us. Help us, Lord, to tap into Your power to pray for those who persecute us, who have hurt us, or who have harmed us or our loved ones. Jesus prayed from the cross for those who had betrayed and harmed Him; help us to find the strength to do the same within our lives. Amen.

Writing: When have you found it difficult to pray for those who harmed you? For those who have hurt you? Write about an experience here. Include your emotions, your thoughts, and if you could fix things, what that fix would be. End your writing with a prayer for the person and situation. Let go of the hurt and anger and leave the rest to God.

Love your enemies and pray for those who persecute you. Matthew 5:44

25 Let God carry the load (Psalm 55:22)

Studies have proven time and again that many of us, including me, carry our stress in our physical bodies. For me, that stress sits squarely on my shoulders and in my neck. Those meditations that tell you to release your shoulders from your ears... I can't really do that exercise. I try, and it's getting better, but my shoulders don't drop much. I've done physical therapy, meditated, exercised, and even taken muscle relaxers to combat the physical symptoms of carrying my stress with me.

I attended a sermon series recently on David and Goliath. This is a story that most Christians know well. I've heard that story since my early childhood and probably in vacation Bible school or after church teachings in the basement of that small church in rural Minnesota. I'm sure I read it in the Bible that one of those teachers gave me and that I still use, cracked binding and all. I know the related songs, including the gestures, and have seen many depictions of this scene. The Psalms of David are poetic and powerful.

David was a shepherd boy, and though he was destined for greatness, he had humble beginnings. He wasn't perfect, and he sinned against God, but that story is for another time. Teenage David brought down a literal giant. A shepherd boy against a nine-foot tall behemoth isn't a fair fight. This sermon series about a familiar story made me think differently about giants, and enemies, and God's plan for those troubles. When God sees an enemy in our lives, He uses it. He helps us fight battles that need to be fought. Goliath wasn't going to stop taunting the Israelites. His leader wasn't going to decide one day that the conflict was over and the armies could all go home. They were locked in a stalemate, and until someone did something, nothing was going to change. Our God is a big God. He equipped 14-year-old David with a sling and a stone, and then he took down a giant standing in the way of God's people.

We don't always get to choose our troubles, our battles, or our enemies. But we do get to choose to ask God for help in those times. Psalm 55:22 tells us to pile our troubles on God's shoulders. With him, we can overcome our challenges, and He will use those times to prepare us for something greater for His glory. Sometimes, we think that the battle is ours, and it isn't. The battle belongs to the Lord. When we stop trying to carry our own troubles and put them on God's shoulders, He helps us move through those challenges to victory on the other side. We can't go around the trouble on our own; we can't run from our problems. We go through the battle, with God's help. We know that God is with us, beside us, behind us, and before us. We can trust that whatever we are facing today, He will see us through, and that the problems are part of His greater plan. We are always going to have trials; we don't have to carry them alone.

Prayer: Lord, thank You for shouldering our burdens and for helping us to find a way. We know that You want to help us; give us the courage to hand over our battles to You. Nothing we face is too great for You. We can praise You in the midst of our storms! Amen.

152

Writing: What are you facing that you need to give to God? Write about your battles here. Pick one or two and write them out, then finish this writing by letting God know how you are piling these troubles onto His shoulders. Ask for God's guidance on how you can let your problems go, knowing that He will help you.

Pile your trouble on God's shoulders. He'll carry your load. He'll help you out.
Psalm 55:22

26 God knows (Proverbs 19:9)

I've mentioned my small town, country upbringing, but you may not realize just how small I am talking about. I grew up on a farm, and the nearest town was four miles away; population, 236. The nearest "big" town, over 25,000 people, was 40 miles away. We were 2.5 hours away from the Minneapolis/St. Paul metropolitan area. My graduating class had 18 students; the school closed five years after I graduated. I went to school with nine of those individuals from kindergarten through 12th grade; in 9th grade, we got nine more students when the parochial school kids joined us. Everyone knew everyone. Quite literally. I can still tell you who in my class didn't like grilled cheese sandwiches; why that fact has stuck with me all this time, I do not know. I'm moved to tears when a friend's parents pass away, even if I haven't seen them in years. These people, these families, these country folk, looked out for each other. When my dad was hurt, they rallied and took care of the farming that year.

Once I was old enough to "go out" on Saturday night, as you can imagine, there weren't a lot of options. Mostly, we went to movies in the big city. And as you can guess, the movie theater didn't have 25 options. I think there were four or five screens. Sometimes we hung out at someone's house and played pool or watched a movie. Sometimes there was a bonfire. And sometimes, well, small-town, rural kids still know this – sometimes you found trouble and ended up where you weren't supposed to be. And of course, your parents found out. Someone in that small town shared the story with them. There were no secrets!

During the winter of my senior year, I was headed to a basketball game, out of town, and driving by myself. I remember that my friends had to work, and I wanted to go, so I did. The weather wasn't cooperating, and it was icier than I realized. My boat of a car did a nice Starsky and Hutch spin on the interstate, and I ended up in the median, facing the wrong way. I drove out of the ditch, got back on the highway, and went to the game. I didn't even spill my Diet Coke (and this was pre-cup holders in cars). Since there was no harm done, to me or to my car, I didn't say anything to my parents. And no, I didn't call them from the ditch. We didn't have cell phones then!

About a week later, my dad and I were watching TV, and he asked if there was anything I wanted to tell him. My brain went into overload; I may or may not have been someplace where I shouldn't have been, but not recently that I could think of? He got around to asking me about the ice skates on my car, and then I knew. The spin on the interstate hadn't been serious, but someone else going to the game had seen me go into the ditch. And since I drove a B-52s style car that sat eight comfortably, those people knew the car and reported the incident to my dad. He was glad I wasn't hurt, and he wasn't angry, but he reminded me to be honest when things like that happened. I don't know why I didn't tell him in the first place. He would have laughed at me not spilling my soda. But I didn't tell him. And I should have.

Proverbs 19:9 reminds us that God knows what we are up to. He knows if we are working in deceit. He knows if we are lying to ourselves or to others. He knows if we are spreading rumors or purposefully trying to harm someone. God knows our hearts. I'm thankful for this, as sometimes when I'm praying, I don't know what to say. The hurt is too big, or the problem seemingly too insurmountable. But God knows what we are thinking and feeling, and He cares for us. He is an awesome God.

Prayer: Lord, sometimes we think we are hiding things from You ... our hurts, our sins, our fears... but You know them already, and we should bring them to You as honestly as we can. Sometimes we don't know what to pray, but You know what is in our hearts, and You will hear our prayers. Time and time again. You will never leave us. Help us to be honest and forthright in all situations. Amen.

Writing: Can you think of a time where you didn't share information that was important, and it later came to light? Write about that time, about your actions and reactions, and why you didn't share. Maybe that has happened to you on the other side of things, where you were left out or not told something. How can we share in the best ways possible? How can we share with God in better ways?

The person who tells lies gets caught; the person who spreads rumors is ruined.
Proverbs 19:9

27 Do not worry (Matthew 6:34)

Even though we've already talked about the futility of worrying, like me, you probably need a reminder. It is important to remember that nowhere in the Bible does God tell us to worry about our lives, our futures, or even what we will eat or drink. God reminds us in His word not to be afraid. He actually does this 365 times throughout the Bible, using phrases like "do not fear" or "do not be afraid." The apostle Paul had plenty of reasons to be afraid. In his letter to the Philippians, Paul was in prison, and he was telling others not to worry. We should probably take note of his circumstances; he's in prison, the outlook for his future is grim, and he's reaching out to those in Philippi to say, "don't worry." In the Book of Matthew, the direction is even more clear. Quit creating worries; you've got enough on your plate today. Tomorrow will take care of itself.

There's an old saying about worry being like a rocking chair; you don't go anywhere, but it gives you something to do. As Christians, we profess that God has our life in His hands. So why are we worrying? What's the point in that? Sometimes (always?) we need to let go of the need for control, of what we want to happen, what we don't want to happen, of how we think things are supposed to go and what the "ending" looks like. We need to get out of God's way. And I know firsthand, that's a tall order for me, and maybe it is for you as well. Those personality tests that give you insight into your preferences? Every test that I've ever taken has mentioned something about liking order over spontaneity, or as one put it, really liking having my ducks in a row. The idea that I can keep ducks in a row is laughable. We can be organized, and we can plan, and we can take steps toward a goal. Many times, we'll achieve those goals. And other times, if what we are working towards is not in God's plan, we will stumble, get off course, and not make it to our destination. Those are the times I've learned to pay attention to more closely. When things aren't going well, is what I'm trying to do aligned with God's plan for my life? Is that why I'm struggling?

When I worried about things growing up, my dad used to tell me that I didn't need to borrow trouble. Sometimes he added "tomorrow is a new day" to his advice. Worrying about our future and what happens next is like that rocking chair. God tells us that He's got us, and that we can trust Him. Can you? Can I? If we are stepping into a new season, we have to step out of the old season, and that can be frightening. We serve a big God. Too often, we see a mountain ahead of us and feel despair. We can take comfort in knowing that God tells that mountain to move and it moves. Nothing is impossible for God. When we are worried, we need to give our worries to God and let them go. Remember when we talked about casting earlier? Let. Them. Go.

Sometimes our fears get the best of us. Sometimes we want to fret and worry and try our best to change our challenging circumstances. We should absolutely do what we can, but we also need to let God be God. We know that God is in charge, and we can stomp our feet and want things to be different when they aren't going our way. But the biggest learning for me was to learn that God's way is always, *always*, the better way. And the sooner I pay attention to redirection and correction, the sooner I arrive where He wants me to be. The challenge for all of us is to let go and let God.

Prayer: Father, we come to You and ask for Your help as we continue our journey. Help us to be still, to not worry, to pray and to thank You for all you've done. Help us to know the peace that comes with understanding that You hold our lives in Your hands, and we do not need to spend energy on worry. You have a bold and wonderful life for us. Help us to refocus and serve You. Amen.

Writing: What are the lessons you have learned about worry that you want to take forward with you? How good are you about giving your worries to God and letting them go? How can you expand on the awareness you've gained to help yourself and others? What can you do the next time you are tempted to worry about tomorrow?

So don't worry about tomorrow; it will have enough worries of its own.
Matthew 6:34

_____

_____

_____

_____

_____

_____

_____

_____

_____

_____

_____

_____

_____

_____

_____

_____

_____

_____

_____

_____

_____

_____

_____

_____

_____

_____

_____

_____

_____

_____

_____

_____

_____

_____

28 Good days are ahead (Jeremiah 29:11)

We are at the end of the journey for this devotional. How are you doing on that be still part? As you look back over the time you've spent reflecting and renewing your spirit, what would you share with someone about your journey? What have you learned that will stay with you in your next season?

I am thankful that you've spent time reading and writing about your relationship with God. Since this is a journey of reflection and renewal, some of you may have really needed the renewal part, as I did when I was writing this journal. Sometimes when we are discouraged, it can feel like we are stuck and we aren't sure how to get unstuck. A large part of my work life has been managing. Managing people. Managing projects. Managing expectations. Managing opportunities. Managing grants. You get the idea. I used the expertise I gained by failing and stumbling, and then I tried to do better in later projects. I created extensive plans, and then I worked those plans. I enjoy creating solutions and helping move things forward to ultimately help people.

Seems like I should be able to do that for my life too, right? That's a false analogy. God knows the plans He has for me. He knows His plan for you as well. I suppose if we really work at it, we can mess up those plans, but I'm doubtful that I'm that powerful. We all can be prideful, arrogant, and willful. God knows this about us, about our flaws, about our character. When we think we have our lives all planned out, life throws us a curveball. A job doesn't materialize. An investment doesn't pan out. Someone gets sick. Someone else's live changes in an instant. Someone passes away much too young. While we know God works all things out for our good, sometimes that doesn't help much as we live our lives, day by day. We want more control.

Or do we?

God's plans for our lives are so much bigger than we can imagine. I know that I've tried to plan and control and manage my own life. I made plans; God had other ideas. Things didn't work out. Other opportunities came along. Life has been extraordinarily full. It isn't perfect, and that's the beauty of life. I know that God's plans are better than mine; and I know that God must have a sense of humor. There have been times when I thought I was travelling along and things were going just as I planned…and then there was a hard left turn I wasn't expecting. I can imagine God saying, "Watch what happens now!"

Perhaps one of the greatest challenges is waiting on God's timing for our lives. Culture tells us that by a certain age, we should be, have, do, or achieve certain things. We can buy into that false story. The Bible is full of God using people throughout their lifetimes, regardless of their flaws and shortcomings, and there is never a time when we are too old to serve others. So, sometimes, it feels like I am being still, waiting, a lot. I pray, I ask for what I think I want, and I wait. I've been working on my patience (another struggle for another day), but I'm confident that if God's plans are bigger and better, He may not answer my prayers exactly. He may have something else in mind for me, something wonderful, and I will embrace life every day. We pray, we wait, and we watch for God's direction, knowing that there is joy ahead!

Prayer: God, thank You for loving us and wanting the best for us. Help us to ask for what we need, Lord, and to be thankful and grateful. Help us to look for Your direction and to be still and listen for Your word. Remind us to be grateful for every day, and to praise Your name while we wait on You. Amen.

Writing: Visualization is a popular strategy. What does your perfect life look life? Have you told God what you want? How has He responded? What has been better than you expected? How can you amp up your prayers? What can you pray for what is outside of yourself? Your family? Your world?

For I know the plans I have for you, declares the Lord, plans to prosper you and not to harm you, plans to give you hope and a future.
Jeremiah 29:11

List of verses in this devotional

Deuteronomy

Deuteronomy 3:22 *Do not be afraid of them; the Lord your God himself will fight for you.*

Deuteronomy 20:4 *The Lord your God is going with you, and He will give you victory.*

James

James 1:6 *But when you pray, you must believe and not doubt at all. Whoever doubts is like a wave in the sea that is driven and blown about by the wind.*

Jeremiah

Jeremiah 29:11 For I know the plans I have for you, declares the Lord, plans to prosper you and not harm you, plans to give you hope and a future.

Hebrews

Hebrews 10:23 *Let us hold unswervingly to the hope we profess, for He who promised is faithful.*

Isaiah

Isaiah 12:2 *God is my savior; I will trust Him and not be afraid. The Lord gives me power and strength; He is my savior.*

Isaiah 43:19 *Look, I am about to do something new; even now it is* *coming. Do you not see it? Indeed, I will make a way in the wilderness; paths in the desert.*

Matthew

Matthew 5:44 *Love your enemies and pray for those who persecute you.*

Matthew 6:34 *So don't worry about tomorrow; it will have enough worries of its own.*

Matthew 11:30 *For my yoke is easy and my burden is light.*

1 Peter

1 Peter 5:7 *God cares for you, so turn all your worries to Him.*

Philippians

Philippians 4:6 *Don't worry about anything: instead pray about everything. Tell God what you need, and thank Him for all He has done.*

Philippians 4:7 *And the peace of God, which surpasses all understanding, will guard your hearts and minds through Christ Jesus.*

Philippians 4:11 *I am not saying this because I am in need, for I have learned to be content whatever the circumstances.*

Proverbs

Proverbs 14:22 *You will earn the respect and trust of others if you work for good...*

Proverbs 19:9 *The person who tells lies gets caught; the person who spreads rumors is ruined.*

Proverbs 19:21 *People may plan all kinds of things, but the Lord's will is going to be done.*

Psalms

Psalm 16:8 *I know the Lord is always with me. I will not be shaken, for He is right beside me.*

Psalm 27:4 *I have asked the Lord for one thing; one thing only do I want: to live in the Lord's house all my life, to marvel there at his goodness and to ask his guidance.*

Psalm 42:11 *Why, my soul, are you downcast? Why so disturbed within me? Put your hope in God, for I will yet praise Him, my Savior and my God.*

Psalm 46:10 *Be still, and know that I am God.*

Psalm 55:22 *Pile your trouble on God's shoulders. He'll carry your load. He'll help you out.*

Psalm 59:1 *Rescue me from my enemies, my God; protect me from those who rise up against me.*

Psalm 121:1 *I lift up my eyes to the mountains; where does my help come from?*

Psalm 126:5 *Those who sow in tears shall reap in joy.*

Romans

Romans 8:28 *And we know that in all things God works for the good of those who love him, who have been called according to his purpose.*

Romans 12:17 *Do not repay anyone evil for evil. Be careful to do what is right in the eyes of everyone.*

1 Samuel
1 Samuel 16:7 *The Lord doesn't see things the way you see them. People judge by outward appearance, but the Lord looks at the heart.*

Thank you!

Thank you for supporting an independent author. If you enjoyed this devotional, **please leave a review** on your favorite site (Amazon, Goodreads, Bookbub, etc.).

Made in the USA
Monee, IL
30 May 2024

59102367R00105